The **Unofficial** Book

Christina
Aguilera

Created in 2000 by
Virgin Books
An imprint of
Virgin Publishing Ltd
Thames Wharf Studios
Rainville Road
London
W6 9HA

First published in the United States in 2000 by Billboard Books, an imprint
of Watson-Guptill Publications, a division of BPI Communications Inc., at 1515
Broadway, New York, NY 10036.

Library of Congress Cataloging-in-Publication Data for this title can be
obtained from the Library of Congress.
Library of Congress Catalog Card Number: 99-69339
ISBN 0 8230 8308 X

Printed and bound by Butler and Tanner Ltd, Frome and London

Designed by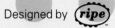

First printing 2000

1 2 3 4 5 6 7 8 9/06 05 04 03 02 01 00

Picture Credits

All Action
Tony Brady 26
Suzan Moore 42, 54
Doug Peters 40, 55
Vinnie Zuffante 23, 56

Famous
Hubert Boesl 38
Fred Duval 13, 41, 48, 51, 59
Paul Fenton 44
Martin Grove 3, 8, 20, 33, 47, 61

Redferns
Paul Bergan 52
Grant Davis 16

Retna
Bill Davila 37, 57
Steve Granitz 39
Walter McBride 53
Leo Sorel 15, 27, 32
Scott Weiner 10

Rex
Brian Rasic 4, 7, 12, 22, 31, 35, 36,
45, 63

South Beach Photo Agency
24

Starfile
Danny Chin 18
Jeffrey Mayer 19, 43, 60
Vinnie Zuffante 17, 28, 30, 49

The **Unofficial** Book

Christina Aguilera

Molly MacDermot

BILLBOARD
BOOKS

Christina Aguilera

Contents

Chapter One

Christina's Wish Comes True

Every once in a while, an artist emerges with a voice so powerful, and so beautiful, that anyone within earshot can't help but be mesmerized by it. Christina Aguilera is one of those gifted singers who has the ability to make magic with her music, and one who has been lucky enough to do so at an early age.

Christina was just two years old when she found her first captive audience – a row of stuffed animals who didn't have much choice but to sit and listen to the young girl sing her first notes. Christina's mother, Shelly, remembers how content Christina was to just stay in her bedroom and belt out songs. When the local kids came over to play, Shelly told them Christina was busy singing, and by the time she was five years old Christina was singing her fave tunes from *The Sound of Music* wherever she went – even on the bus! Christina has said that she still smiles when she thinks back to those early days, and even jokes that she must have seemed like a pretty weird kid. Well, that "weird" kid with the uncontrollable urge to sing turned into a phenomenally successful artist with a number one album by the time she was just eighteen years old.

Christina will never forget the day her debut album hit stores for the first time. It was August 24, 1999, and Christina was spending the hot summer day in a Los Angeles record store, happily signing albums for a long line of fans. Christina has said that she felt completely overwhelmed and amazed, because just a short time ago she had walked into that very record store to buy some CDs and wondered when her own music would be on the shelves. Now it was really happening.

Christina's album went gold within a week of its release, selling an astonishing 252,800 copies

Christina's album went gold within a week of its release, selling an astonishing 252,800 copies, outstripping Puff Daddy's highly anticipated new album *Forever* by almost 50,000 copies. Christina's number one position on the *Billboard* record charts meant that regulars like the Backstreet Boys, who had been number one almost all summer, and other heavyweights such as Ricky Martin and Limp Bizkit, were bumped down the chart to make room for the newcomer. Who would have thought that this new girl on the block would blow everyone else away with her tunes? Christina has said that even now she can't believe she debuted at number one and wonders if maybe they made a mistake when they added up the numbers.

Well, there definitely was no mistake. Christina dominated the number one spot for five weeks, her video for "Genie In A Bottle" was one of the most requested on MTV's popular show *Total Request Live*, and magazines and newspapers throughout the country were dubbing her the "voice of her generation." Not bad for an eighteen-year-old from Pittsburgh who had graduated from high school a month before "Genie In A Bottle" was released.

Some music industry insiders have compared Christina with divas like Mariah Carey, Whitney Houston and Barbra Streisand because her voice has that rare combination of maturity, soul, and attitude – a rarity in someone so young. But unlike these high-maintenance divas, this blonde beauty with the big blue eyes and booming voice is still a carefree, fun-loving teen. For starters, she's got teen taste buds, and is a big fan of fast-food restaurants like Wendy's and McDonald's. She also has boys on the brain and admits she's crazy for crushes Enrique Iglesias and Eminem. And, like any girl her age, Christina loves to chat with her friends, which might explain why she can't live without her precious red cell phone.

While some critics are quick to call her a Britney Spears clone, Christina – who is friends with Britney from their days together on the *New Mickey Mouse Club* – thinks the comparison is naive. Although both performers love to sing and dance, close listeners can hear that Christina's unique style is influenced by rhythm and blues, not pop. But true Christina fans already knew that.

Christina has said that even now she can't believe she debuted at number one and wonders if maybe they made a mistake when they added up the numbers

Ten Things You Didn't Know About Christina

1 Christina's nickname is X-Tina. One of the guys at her record company thought it would be cute to shorten her name in the same way Christmas is shortened to "X-mas."

2 "Genie In A Bottle" almost didn't make the album. The song, written by David Frank and Steve Kipner, who also wrote the 98 Degrees song "The Hardest Thing," wasn't presented to Christina until her album was practically finished. Plus, Christina wasn't crazy about the song until she added her own personal touches in the studio. She originally wanted to showcase her voice with a big ballad like Mariah Carey's 1990 debut, "Vision of Love." Good thing she gave "Genie..." a chance.

3 Even though the video for "Genie In a Bottle" was shot in Malibu, California, the weather that day was very cold. While the crew bundled in coats and scarves, Christina had to loll on the beach in shorts. What a trooper!

4 Christina grew up loving *The Sound of Music*, but she soon discovered that not everyone shared her passion. During a interview, an reporter told Christina that *The Sound of Music* gave her nightmares. Christina couldn't believe such melodic music could actually scare someone.

5 Talking of being scared, Christina hates the dark. She sleeps with the lights on.

6 It was Christina's idea to include the radio-compressed speaking parts in "Genie In A Bottle." What a cool hook!

7 If Christina could be an animal, she has said she'd be a cat, because she can be quiet one moment and full of energy the next.

8 Christina's most over-used word is "cute" – she says it all the time!

9 Christina's all-time fave albums are Janet Jackson's *Control*, Fugees' *The Score*, Madonna's *The Immaculate Collection*, Mariah Carey's *Mariah Carey* and Brian McKnight's *Brian McKnight*.

10 Christina likes to be in the spotlight. When she was a kid, a family friend came to the house to show his paintings, and spread them on the floor. To attract attention, little Christina played hopscotch on the works of art.

Christina Loves...

Female singers: Mariah Carey, Madonna, Lauryn Hill, Whitney Houston, Julie Andrews and Etta James

Male singers: Michael Jackson, Brian McKnight

Band: Boyz II Men, No Doubt, Eve 6, Limp Bizkit

Drink: Nestle Quick chocolate milk, milk, Coke

Food: Bacon cheeseburgers, chicken nuggets with mustard sauce, fries topped with chili and cheese

Sport: Baseball

Subjects: English, Science

Hobbies: Shopping, going to the movies, hanging with friends, dancing

Movies: *Mulan, The Little Mermaid*

TV show: MTV's *Total Request Live*

Essentials

Date of birth: December 18, 1980

Sign: Sagittarius

Compatible with: Leo

Siblings: Rachel, Casey, Stephanie, Robert Michael

Tattoos: She doesn't have any

She writes with her: Right hand

Secret indulgence: French manicures

Christina and Britney

As most fans know, Christina and Britney Spears have been friends since they first met on *The New Mickey Mouse Club*. After the show ended, the friends went their separate ways, Christina to Pennsylvania and Britney to Louisiana, and kept in touch with letters. So, now that they're both famous, is it true that they're rivals? Not at all. In fact, Christina has said that when Britney's album ...*Baby One More Time* first came out on January 12, 1999, she was the first one in line to buy it. She even thought about calling radio stations to request Britney's music, but realized they were already playing it. Although she admits they're both extremely busy and it's sometimes hard to stay in touch, she has said she will continue to support Britney because that's what friends do.

There are some uncanny similarities between Christina Aguilera and Britney Spears. Fans, of course, know that each artist has her own personal style and sound, but here's a quick rundown on what they do share that even the biggest fans might not know.

Small town values: Christina grew up in Wexford, Pennsylvania and Britney grew up in Kentwood, Louisiana, both small towns where everyone knows each other.
Born performers: Both Christina and Britney expressed their love for singing at an early age. Before they were introduced to the microphone, Christina used to sing into her shampoo bottle, while Britney used to sing into her hairbrush.
Talent show tots: Mothers know their daughters best, and both Christina's mother Shelly and Britney's mother Lynne knew their daughters wouldn't be happy unless they were performing, so they signed them up in local talent shows. In fact, both girls performed on *Star Search* when they were eight years old.
The New Mickey Mouse Club: It seems like many performers today have spent at least some time as a Mouseketeer, including Christina and Britney. In fact, both girls didn't get their mouse ears the first time they auditioned because they were too young. They both landed a spot on the show after they auditioned a second time, and it was on the *MMC* set that the two youngest cast members finally met.

Both Christina's mother Shelly and Britney's mother Lynne knew their daughters wouldn't be happy unless they were performing

Dinky demos: Both girls recorded their demo tapes at home on cheap tape recorders. And both landed record deals soon after.

Whitney Houston fans: Christina and Britney loved listening to Whitney Houston when they were growing up, so it makes sense that they both chose Whitney's songs for their big auditions. Christina sang "Run To You" and got the *Mulan* gig; Britney sang "I Have Nothing" and got a record contract with Jive. Perhaps Whitney brings good luck.

Chart-toppers: Both Christina and Britney had debut albums that stayed at number one on the *Billboard* record charts. They're two of the biggest selling teen girls of all time.

Astrological twins: Both girls are born under the sign of Sagittarius. Christina was born on December 18, 1980; Britney was born on December 2, 1981.

Sweet successes: Christina and Britney are both going to be around for a long time. They've both made guest appearances on television; Christina was on *Beverly Hills 90210*; Britney was on *Dawson's Creek*; both have received numerous movie offers, and both girls want to continue pleasing their fans with many more new albums!

Both have received numerous movie offers, and both girls want to continue pleasing their fans with many more new albums!

Chapter Two

The Little Girl With The Big Voice

There's no denying that Christina is a particularly petite performer – she's only 5 feet 2 inches in platforms. They say that good things come in small packages – and that's certainly true of Christina, whose surprisingly powerful voice can carry to the very back row of a huge auditorium. According to friends and family, she's always been a little girl with a big voice, even when she was a pint-sized ten-year-old singing the National Anthem for her home football team, the Pittsburgh Steelers.

She's also a little girl with a big name. Christina Maria Aguilera (pronounced A-ghe-lera) used to be difficult to remember until it became a household name. Way before her name was topping the charts, Christina lived a normal life like most girls her age. She was born on December 18, 1980 in Staten Island, New York, a family-friendly borough that's just a ferry ride away from downtown Manhattan. She was the first born to parents Fausto, an Ecuadorian Army Sergeant, and Shelly, an Irish-American violinist. Because her dad was in the army, the Aguileras moved around a lot, which meant Christina was constantly the new girl in school, whether she was living in Texas, Japan or New Jersey. Her parents had another daughter, Rachel, but separated when Christina was seven years old.

It was at that time that Shelly moved with her

two daughters to live with their grandmother in Wexford, Pennsylvania, a town outside of Pittsburgh where the close-knit family still resides. Although Christina recently bought an apartment on the Upper West Side in New York City, she has said she still likes to visit her basement room in Wexford – which contains Christina's most prized possession, her lava lamp. Christina's mother later met Jim, a paramedic, and remarried. Christina has two step-brothers, Casey and Robert Michael, and one step-sister, Stephanie. Growing up with four

She's always been a little girl with a big voice, even when she was a pint-sized ten-year-old singing the National Anthem for her home football team

Growing up with four other siblings has made Christina well-adjusted; she knows how to laugh at herself even when people try to put her on a pedestal because she's a star

other siblings has made Christina well-adjusted; she knows how to laugh at herself even when people try to put her on a pedestal because she's a star. She remembers one especially embarrassing moment growing up when she was playing baseball – a sport she loves – with her brother Casey. Christina was accidentally hit in the jaw with the baseball, and her face swelled up to an enormous size. Being the tomboy that she was, she shrugged her shoulders and carried on with the game.

Christina grew especially close to her grandmother when she moved in with her at the age of seven, and remembers one particularly happy childhood memory. It was during the Christmas holidays, and like most little girls her age she was wishing hard for a Barbie kitchen. She had the surprise of her life when she went downstairs on Christmas Day and saw that her grandmother had the gift waiting for her.

Aside from material goods, Christina's grandmother gave her the most precious gift of all when she advised young Christina to always follow her dreams – an inspiration Christina holds dear to this day. Her grandmother noticed that Christina had an ear for singing, so she exposed her to blues music. They'd spend

quality time together at used record stores, searching out albums by blues singers Billie Holiday and Etta James – two women Christina continues to find inspiration from to this day. She particularly loves to perform Etta James' song "At Last," which she sang at Lilith Fair in 1999.

Christina's mother has said that when Christina was growing up she would get cranky if she wasn't singing, so she let the little performer participate in talent shows and block parties. When Christina sang Whitney Houston's "I Wanna Dance with Somebody" in her first-grade talent show to an impressed audience of five- and six-year-olds, she discovered she really liked performing and wanted more. She performed at more and more parties and events, and remembers people rushing to the stage to get her autograph. She admits she's always loved getting attention, and unlike some stars who shun their fans, Christina doesn't mind being stopped on the street by admirers to chat or sign autographs. After all, she has said, it's her fans who have made all of this success possible.

It didn't take long for the ambitious Christina to grow bored performing at block parties and talent shows, so when she was eight years old she took a big step and tried out on *Star Search*, a nationally televised talent show which showcases up-and-coming stars. Accompanied by her mother, Christina hopped on a plane and took her first trip to glamorous Los Angeles, where the show was being taped. It was an exciting time for Christina, because she was finally getting a glimpse of Hollywood, a place she had always dreamed about.

At eight years old she took a big step and tried out on Star Search, a nationally televised talent show which showcases up-and-coming stars

The judges were impressed with her near-flawless rendition of Whitney Houston's heartwarming song "The Greatest Love of All," but the competition was fierce. Unfortunately, Christina would receive her first taste of disappointment when the grand prize was awarded to a twelve-year-old boy who sang Eddie Holman's "Hey There Lonely Girl." She has said it was a devastating moment that she still replays in her head, because she had so desperately wanted to win. Even though she had tears running down her cheeks, she was a good sport and followed her mother's gracious suggestion by congratulating the winner. Christina has said in interviews that she wonders sometimes what became of the boy who denied her the grand prize. No doubt he's amazed at how far his competition has come. Christina kept her chin up and used her runner-up's winnings to buy a portable radio so she could sing along to it in the park.

The *Star Search* experience also taught Christina an invaluable lesson about the pitfalls that can accompany stardom. After seeing Christina on television, schoolmates grew resentful of her budding career, and she soon became the object of ridicule. Christina tried to ignore their snubs, but it was hurtful. When her mother's car was vandalized, she had reached her limit and transferred to another school. She has said that singing is a good way for her to release any "bad energy" that she's feeling, so when she's unhappy she turns to music for comfort. Music is in her blood – her mother is a trained violinist who toured Europe with the Youth Symphony Orchestra when she was sixteen years old. Christina has said that when she's busy on the road and can't always call home, her mother reminds her that she did the same thing when she was a teen.

After seeing Christina on television, schoolmates grew resentful of her budding career

In 1990, just when Christina was trying to find her musical calling, a new artist named Mariah Carey came on the scene with her debut album and the soaring ballad "Vision of Love." As soon as she heard it, Christina was in awe of Mariah's voice and has said it was truly a "breath of fresh air." Grunge and gangsta rap had been dominating the airwaves, so it was a relief to hear an artist bringing back the big ballads. Christina remembers asking her mother if she'd ever sing like the powerful diva. Little did she know she'd be heralded as the next Mariah several years later.

One day, Christina's mother read in the local newspaper that there was an open casting call for the *New Mickey Mouse Club*. Disney's nationally televised variety show, first shown in the 1950s, was making a big comeback, and they were looking for new talent. Without missing a beat, Christina and her mother drove to Pittsburgh for the audition. Although nine-year-old Christina didn't get cast at the time because she was too young, she made a good impression on the producers. The show called her up two years later to say they had kept her audition tape and asked whether she would be interested in auditioning again for one of the six new openings on the show. Christina jumped at the chance, and this time she sealed the deal by showing off her vastly improved talents – she was, after all, a whole two years older. They loved her and offered her the coveted role as a Mouseketeer that day. Life was taking an exciting turn for the songbird-in-training.

Christina moved with her mother to an apartment in Orlando, where the show was filmed, and soon discovered she had finally found a group of friends her age who shared her passion for performing. She felt at home and loved the camaraderie of her fellow crew mates, who included the talented Britney Spears, Justin Timberlake and J.C. Chasez (who would later form 'N Sync), and Keri Russell (now the star of

The show was a learning experience she'll never forget, and full of memorable moments, like the time she had a pie thrown in her face!

Christina remembers asking her mother if she'd ever sing like the powerful diva. Little did she know she'd be heralded as the next Mariah several years later

top TV show *Felicity*), among others. She smiles when she thinks back to those days and remembers how she was one of the babies on the show, along with Justin (who is the same age as her) and Britney (who is one year younger). She remembers looking up to Keri Russell, then sixteen, and thinking she was the epitome of cool with her long corkscrew curls, frayed jeans and sports car. She has said she was sure Keri would turn out to be a glamour gal, but instead she plays a modest college student on *Felicity*. The show was a learning

experience she'll never forget, and full of memorable moments, like the time she had a pie thrown in her face! She has said that even then she knew that each of her fellow Mouseketeers would go on to greater success.

After spending two seasons on the show, the relentless singing, dancing and acting had made her a well-rounded performer. While she was on the show, Christina was spotted by her manager Steve Kurtz. Christina would later thank him in her album notes for "caring about me as a person and always going the extra mile."

When the *New Mickey Mouse Club* was shelved in October 1994, Christina turned to new projects, including a trip to Japan.

Japanese fans already knew her from the *New Mickey Mouse Club*, and she made an even bigger splash when she recorded a duet titled "All I Wanna Do" with the popular Japanese star Keizo Nakanishi. She had her first taste of life on the road when she toured Japan, and later that year she visited Transylvania, Romania – home of the fictional Count Dracula. Aside from visiting Dracula's scary castle (He was based on a real person, she learned), Christina joined artists like Sheryl Crow and Diana Ross at Transylvania's famous Golden Stag Festival. Although she performed in front of an overwhelming 10,000 people, she gave them a fearless performance and even mustered the confidence to wade through the huge crowd as she sang.

Chapter Three

The Note That Changed Her Life

Christina's career was about to get the jump-start it needed. After touring Japan, she returned home even more eager to pursue her musical career. She was happy to have recorded a duet with Keizo Nakanishi, but she still dreamed of recording her own album and felt that now was the time.

Christina still remembers the details of the day her career took a dramatic turn. She was kicking back at home in Wexford when the telephone rang. It was her manager calling with some big news. He had sent Christina's demo tape to Ron Fair, an A&R (artist and repertoire) executive at RCA Records who had worked with many famous artists, including Natalie Cole and the O'Jays. Ron was so impressed with Christina's voice that he held on to the tape. At about the same time as he discovered Christina's demo tape, Ron received a phone call from an executive at Disney who needed a young voice to sing the lead song on the soundtrack for *Mulan*, Disney's 36th animated feature film, and wondered if Ron had any suggestions. Ron, who hadn't yet signed Christina to RCA Records, quickly phoned Christina's manager, who just as frantically called Christina to see if she'd be interested in

singing on the *Mulan* soundtrack. She just happened to be home when the phone rang, and boy was she thrilled to get the call!

There was one big requirement for the job. Disney needed to know if she could hit the right note – a high E above middle C. Christina rushed to her piano to try and match the note, and was pleasantly surprised to discover she could do it. Now she just had to prove it to Disney, so she grabbed her cheap tape recorder and sang Whitney Houston's "Run To Me" on her

Disney needed to know if she could hit the right note – a high E above middle C. Christina rushed to her piano to try and match the note

Just 24 hours after she had sent her tape – and 3,000 miles later – Christina was auditioning before producer Matthew Wilder in the studio bathroom floor. Christina has said that the bathroom had the best acoustics in the house, and as she didn't have a ready-made recording studio, the bathroom was the next best thing. She sent the tape overnight to Disney's Los Angeles headquarters and waited nervously for their reaction.

Christina has often turned to Whitney Houston songs during crossroads in her career. First it was Whitney's "I Wanna Dance With Somebody" for her first talent show, then it was "The Greatest Love Of All" for *Star Search*, and now "Run To You" from *The Bodyguard* soundtrack was being pressed into service to secure Christina her big break. Would three be her lucky number? The very next day she got a call asking her to fly to Los Angeles immediately. What was about to happen would be a total shock to Christina.

Wasting no time, Christina hopped a plane, just as she had done when she was going to perform on *Star Search*. Just 24 hours after she had sent her tape – and 3,000 miles later – Christina was auditioning before producer Matthew Wilder in the studio. Making sure to

put her nerves aside, Christina gave it all she had and sang the best she could. He couldn't believe his ears – how could someone so young sing so powerfully? He offered her the job on the spot. The next day she was recording the *Mulan* theme song, "Reflection" and the day after that she was signing a record deal with RCA Records.

Christina has said she couldn't believe her luck, because not only was she singing on a Disney soundtrack, but she had a record deal! She had never done so much singing in such a short space of time. She ended up working all week in the studio to get the recording of "Reflection" perfect, and she even received her first voice lesson. If Disney hadn't taken a chance with an unknown talent, Christina wouldn't have got the break she had been dreaming of her whole life. After she finished recording "Reflection," Christina stayed to hear a 90-piece orchestra record the accompaniment to her singing. She remembers feeling an overwhelming sense of awe listening to the orchestra play her song, and she burst into tears.

The soundtrack to *Mulan* was released on June 2, 1998 and "Reflection" reached the Top 15 on the Adult/Contemporary music charts. It was also nominated for a Golden Globe for best original song in a motion picture, and an ALMA (American Latino Media Arts Award).

Mulan is about a Chinese girl who disguises herself as a warrior to save her aging father from going to war. She's a strong, independent, spirited girl, who represents the same "girl power" Christina strives for. Christina has said it was amazing to actually hear her own song as the credits rolled after the movie. It really was an appropriate song for Christina's grand entrance into the music world, because the song is about the struggle to establish an identity – something Christina could really relate to.

Mulan is a strong, independent, spirited girl, who represents the same "girl power" Christina strives for

Christina Aguilera

Christina was just beginning to ride the wave of her success. She wasted little time getting to work on her debut album with RCA, which was recorded mostly during the summer of 1998 in Los Angeles. Although Christina was far from home and had to adjust to living in a hotel, she was having the time of her life. She worked with a number of impressive songwriters, like the prolific Diane Warren, who has written some of the biggest songs of the past twenty years, including hits for Celine Dion, 'N Sync and Aerosmith. She remembers how fun it was to work with Diane on the inspirational ballad "I Turn To You." Diane's dry wit and jokes in the studio would frequently cause Christina to crack up with laughter, even though the serious ballad they were recording was no laughing matter!

Christina was nearing the completion of her album when a certain song landed on her producer's desk. It was called "Genie In A Bottle," and although he knew it was going to be a hit, he had to persuade Christina. She has said that she was concerned it sounded too "pop," and that it didn't properly showcase her wide vocal range and R&B style. After a little convincing from her producer, and some reworking from Christina in the studio, she agreed to include it on the album. It would end up being her first single and her first number one on the charts.

Although Christina was far from home and had to adjust to living in a hotel, she was having the time of her life

Chapter Four

One Crazy Carpet Ride

Although Christina worked on her debut album in 1998, it wasn't released until August 24, 1999. She remembers waiting eagerly for the album to come out, and has recalled watching Britney Spears and 'N Sync on MTV's Total Request Live, anxiously wondering when it would be her turn.

The wait was worth it. Once her music hit the airwaves that memorable summer, the swelling sales of "Genie in a Bottle" sealed Christina's status as the new singing sensation of the year.

Accompanied by a piano, she performed at Lilith Fair, the world famous all-girl music festival started by Sarah McLachlan. She performed with pop singer Joey McIntyre at the Greek Theatre in Los Angeles, and hosted MTV's *Total Request Live* in New York's Times Square. Fans flooded the sidewalks outside MTV's headquarters holding homemade poster boards to show their support.

She treated fans to a guest appearance on *Beverly Hills 90210*, and soon she was receiving invitations to attend star-studded events like the MTV Video Music Awards, where she presented an award with bad boy Tommy Lee, the former drummer of Motley Crue and husband of Pamela Anderson. She was also asked to

perform on several popular television talk shows, including *The Late Show With David Letterman* and *The Tonight Show with Jay Leno*. The Christina craze was just beginning – there was even a Christina collectible doll that sang "Genie In A Bottle." As 1999 was drawing to a close and people were getting ready for the new millennium, life was getting even more crazy for Christina. She had a schedule totally packed with fun events, and this busy girl was literally flying from one continent to the next.

As 1999 was drawing to a close and people were getting ready for the new millennium, life was getting even more crazy for Christina.

On November 11 she attended the European MTV Awards in Dublin, Ireland; on November 21 she flew to Boston to perform at the Major League Soccer Final, which drew thousands of viewers: and on November 25 she walked with the famous floats in the Macy's Thanksgiving Day Parade in New York. She also released her version of "The Christmas Song" and had fans singing "chestnuts roasting on an open fire" along with her for the holidays.

If that wasn't enough for one person to handle, she also attended the Billboard Music Awards in Las Vegas on December 8, celebrated her nineteenth birthday on December 18, and ushered in the new millennium with MTV in Times Square, New York. Without much time to catch up on sleep, Christina was a guest at the *Ladies' Home Journal* "Most Fascinating Women of the Year" event on January 3.

Life took yet another an exciting turn when Christina started her January tour opening for chart-toppers TLC. She performed before thousands of screaming fans and the energy was electric, whether she was singing at Madison Square Garden in New York, or at the

Mandalay Bay Arena in Las Vegas. This genie was on one crazy carpet ride she'll never forget.

Although she admits life as a superstar can be incredibly draining, it is the fans' enthusiasm and energy that keeps her going. For example, she remembers feeling sick the day she had to perform in front of 18,000 fans for L'Oréal's Summer Music Mania Madness concert, which aired on UPN. Yet, once she saw the cheering crowd and started her performance, she instantly felt better.

The crowd felt pretty great, too, because Christina is known for putting on an amazing live performance. She has said that when she has one chance to wow an audience she gets a jolt of adrenaline that's just intense. She prefers the energy of a live band to pre-recorded tracks, because she can do more interesting things with a song. For "Genie In A Bottle," she sometimes adds Arabian-style intonations

Although she admits life as a superstar can be incredibly draining, it is the fans' enthusiasm and energy that keeps her going

throughout the song to put the audience into a Middle Eastern mood. She also likes to try different beats for "What A Girl Wants" to make sure the audience is surprised every once in a while. She has said she wouldn't like to lip-sync at a concert, although she knows it can be difficult for an artist to sing and dance at the same time.

As any star soon discovers, with success comes a whirlwind of changes. Suddenly everyone recognizes you, and you have more pressures piled on you than you ever imagined. Christina loves meeting her fans and truly appreciates their support in all that she does. She has said that she feels terrible when she can't give autographs to everyone, but sometimes it's just too difficult when the crowd is so huge. There are cases, however, when the frenzy of fans gets out of control. She remembers one crazy moment when a group of fans nearly drove her off the road. She was in a rush to get to a television interview, and some fans were waiting for her by the car. As soon as she got in, they jumped in their cars and started chasing her. Christina tries to avoid scary situations like this as much as she possibly can.

Being recognized does have its perks at times, however. She remembers shopping for makeup in Japan, when a group of girls spotted the singer and screamed out her name for everyone to hear. She ended up getting a big discount on the makeup!

As any star soon discovers, with success comes a whirlwind of changes

Christina has said she tries to keep a positive outlook at all times, and admits she's a bit of a control freak because she hates feeling the least bit vulnerable

Christina also remembers some moments in her new career that left her completely mortified, like the time she was having dinner with some bigwig record executives in Toronto, Canada. She tried to be as poised and presentable as possible, but discovered that it's not always easy. On her way to her table she didn't see a glass door in her way – she slammed right into it and fell to the floor in front of the whole restaurant!

To stay sane when life is anything but, Christina takes a relaxing hot bubble bath after a long day, and lets her mind daydream. What some fans may not know is that Christina actually has a quiet, eccentric side and she usually spends much of her downtime doing some serious thinking. She is also spiritual and prays regularly.

Christina has said she tries to keep a positive outlook at all times, and admits she's a bit of a control freak because she hates feeling the least bit vulnerable. She likes to read books about following your dreams and believes that if you're passionate about something, work hard and follow your heart, you can make your dreams come true. Every year on her birthday she throws a coin in a fountain for good luck, and has said that if she had three wishes, she'd wish for a driver's license, (her younger brother teases her because she doesn't have one and he does), a little sports car and a long-lasting career. She remembers wishing on a star back home that she'd be a star herself one day. Well, it looks like this genie is rubbing good fortune the right way.

Chapter Five

Christina's Secret Crush

Naturally, everyone is curious about Christina's love life because she belts out such beautiful love ballads. There must be a certain sweetie somewhere in the audience who inspires this emotion. For now, Christina is single, but she's not shy about her swoon-worthy crushes. After all, a girl can dream, can't she?

As the saying goes, birds of a feather flock together, and in Christina's case it couldn't be more true – this singing sensation has said she's often smitten for other singers like herself, especially if they have a little edge and fit the rock'n'roll type. First she had a crush on pretty boy Mark McGrath from the band Sugar Ray, but Christina concluded he was too cocky for her. Then she had eyes for rebel rapper Eminem, although she admits she doesn't usually go for blondes. She even thought bad boy turned good boy Robbie Williams would make a good boyfriend. Now it's sultry singer Enrique Iglesias who grabs her fancy because he has the feature Christina loves – a sweet smile.

One reason Christina has crushes on other performers is because they would be more likely to relate to her crazy schedule than someone who isn't in the business. It's often very difficult for superstars to enjoy much of a personal life, because they're always flying from one city to the next and don't have the time to get to really know a person. Christina has said that she would make time for a boyfriend if she met someone special. For now, she's content to wait for Mr. Right.

So what does this girl really want? Christina's a free-spirited Sagittarius who needs her space, and as she says in her song "What A Girl Wants," "I wanna thank you for giving me time to breathe." She has said she also likes a guy

Enrique Iglesias grabs her fancy because he has the feature Christina loves – a sweet smile.

who is artistic, unique and stands out in a crowd. Boring guys with zero originality need not apply. That's not too much to ask, right? For instance, if she's watching a movie, she usually falls for the quirky actor that no one has ever heard of.

When it comes down to catching a cutie's attention, Christina likes to play hard to get. She has a specific walk she uses to snag a sweetie's attention, she has said, and her dancers tease her about it mercilessly. The walk trick is pretty simple – she subtly sways her hips while she goes past a guy, then she glances back to see his reaction. Although she admits she's hard to get in the beginning, she doesn't like playing games. Once a guy proves himself and she knows his feelings are sincere, she'll give him a chance. As she says in her song "Genie In A Bottle," she has no time for guys who are cool and reserved – if they can't rise to the challenge, she's just not interested.

Christina has said that she would make time for a boyfriend if she met someone special. For now, she's content to wait for Mr. Right.

Chapter Six

 True Friends

No one understands the true meaning of friendship like Christina. From an early age, this ambitious kid learned how important it is to hold on to close pals. She experienced cold glares from classmates after she performed on *Star Search*, and eventually had to transfer to another school.

Christina ended up being home-schooled and tutored while she fulfilled her musical ambitions, but she never forgot the taunts from jealous peers. She faced the same wrath when she attended her high school prom in the spring of 1999. Her best friend Marcy urged her to go, but Christina was hesitant. After all, how would her peers react to her new-found fame? After some coaxing, Christina agreed to attend the prom; Marcy set her up with a blind date, but Christina had already promised to go with a guy friend. In order not to hurt anyone's feelings, she went to the prom with both guys.

Unfortunately, Christina predicted right about the other students, because when she arrived she didn't exactly receive a friendly welcome. "Genie In A Bottle" had just been released and was everywhere on the radio, and when the DJ played it the dancefloor cleared. Apparently, jealousy was an issue and only two girls came up to her to talk that night; the others were standing by their boyfriends, refusing to make an effort.

It's hard for anyone to avoid classroom clashes, let alone someone who seems different from the others. While in school, Christina was much more interested in pursuing music than running the school newspaper or being the captain of the cheerleading team.

Christina was much more interested in pursuing music than running the school newspaper or being the captain of the cheerleading team

Christina learned how to weed out the phony friends from her life, and continues to do so. Now she only surrounds herself with supportive friends who stand by her

She has said she couldn't get away with having a bad day like other kids, because if she did one thing wrong, everyone would notice. It meant she had to grow up faster and be stronger.

Christina learned how to weed out the phony friends from her life, and continues to do so. Now she only surrounds herself with supportive friends who stand by her – and who like to have fun, of course. This spunky girl loves bonding with her buds, so when she has a moment free from her busy schedule to breathe, she enjoys going to the movies, shopping and chatting with her girlfriends.

Christina's closest friend is her mother, who runs Christina's fan club and keeps her posted on what her fans are saying. She has said that it takes a brave mother to allow her daughter to pursue a showbiz career, and she is forever grateful for the support she gets from her family.

What Christina has discovered is that she has gained hundreds of thousands of new friends – her fans. She likes to surf the web to stay informed about her ever-growing fan base, and she plans on getting a laptop so she can keep in touch with fans and friends when she's on the road. She receives loads of friendly letters from fans all over the world who write to say she inspires and encourages them to pursue their own dreams, and has said that there is no better feeling in the world like having people support you like that. The thing she loves most about being a star – and what really gives her the chills – is hearing the audience singing along with every word by heart.

Chapter Seven

She's Stylin'

It's always fun to see what Christina's going to wear because she loves to follow fashion and try the new trends. She looks up to fashion divas like Madonna and Janet Jackson who aren't afraid to experiment with far-out fabrics and cutting edge designs. She has said that she admires the way they always have something creative and new to offer the public, whether it's with their music or their clothes. When it's time to get fancy, Christina wears daring outfits by Italian designers Dolce & Gabbana and Moschino. She's a fan of faux fur, like zebra and leopard prints, and likes to add her own girlie charm with cheery pink or red splashes.

Christina was in her fashion element when she joined host Rebecca Romijn-Stamos on MTV's *House of Style* to introduce the fabulous fall coats for 1999. She had the fun job of trying the top designers' cool creations for the new season.

For the 1999 MTV Video Music Awards, Christina wore a leopard-print top with electric pink lace trim, a leopard-print coat, a cute black miniskirt and ultra-cool black platform boots. She accessorized with sparkling earrings and a gem necklace. For the 1999 Teen Choice Awards, Christina lit up the red carpet wearing a

vintage poncho inspired by the designs of South America. She completed the outfit with an elegant black skirt, strappy sandals and silver hoop earrings.

In her videos, she likes to wear bright, fun outfits that scream "cool." The orange pants she wears in the video for "Genie In A Bottle" were one of the most requested items at Abercrombie & Fitch. Although it's hard to see in the video, there's actually a huge dragon on the lower left leg.

When she's performing on stage she shows a gutsy glam-rock edge, with black leather pants and ultra-bright tops. She's especially fond of bellybutton-flashing midriffs, tube tops, and tank tops in fire engine reds, tie-dye pinks, and swimming pool blues that match her eyes.

Christina wears daring outfits by Italian designers Dolce & Gabbana and Moschino. She's a fan of faux fur, like zebra and leopard prints

She's a perfectionist about her long nails – one bad habit she doesn't suffer from is nail biting – so she makes them gorgeous with a French manicure

To add a few inches to her petite frame, Christina usually wears platform shoes, although they can be tough to dance in.

Christina also loves to accessorize with funky armlets, belly necklaces and thumb rings. Her latest find? Leather or sequin-covered wristbands. Of course, on her days off, Christina ditches the designer clothes and opts for super comfy clothes, like jeans, T-shirts, and sneakers. She loves dressing up but she knows it's important to kick back and dress down when you can.

When it comes to beauty, this photogenic genie knows how to make magic with her makeup. To even out her skin tone, Christina dabs concealer under her eyes and over her blemishes (even famous faces break out sometimes!). Then she smooths a light foundation on her skin, and applies rose-tinted blush to the apples of her cheeks.

She dusts her eyelids with shimmer-packed pink eye shadow, which brings out her bright blue eyes, and for added eye drama Christina curls her eyelashes and coats them twice with black mascara. To add flirty femininity to her now famous pout, Christina slicks on pink pastel lip-gloss. If she's feeling adventurous, she lines her lips and fills them in with candy-apple-red lipstick – like she wore on her album cover.

She's a perfectionist about her long nails – one bad habit she doesn't suffer from is nail biting – so she makes them gorgeous with a French manicure. When it comes to taking care of her hair, Christina's got blonde ambitions. Naturally an ash blonde, she likes to lighten her locks for a livelier look. To pump up her fine hair, she uses an extra-body spray volumizer. Then, depending on her mood, she either blow dries her hair straight with a big metal round brush, which retains heat for better styling, or she lets it dry naturally for a tousled, bed-head look. For fun, she gives herself a zig-zag parting and runs a serum or glosser through her hair to flatten flyaways and add shine. Try the same beauty steps at home and – voilà! – you've got instant star style!

Chapter Eight

21st Century Girl

It's appropriate that Christina welcomed in the new millennium with MTV, because she's unveiling a whole bunch of exciting projects for the new century that should satisfy music fans everywhere.

To get in touch with her South American roots, she is studying Spanish and recording a Spanish album in Miami with veteran producer Rudy Perez, who has worked with Marc Anthony, Julio Iglesias and many other talented singers. The album features a string of sassy songs and includes a new version of "Genie In A Bottle" or, as it's said in Spanish, "Genio Atrapado." Christina has always had a love for Latin culture, and when fans came up to her and started speaking Spanish she knew she had to learn the language better and get in touch with that part of herself. Of course, Latin music is gaining lots of attention now with artists like Ricky Martin, Jennifer Lopez, and Enrique and Julio Iglesias Jr topping the charts, but Christina doesn't want to pigeonhole herself and just be known as a Latin artist. She wants to continue to sing songs that are universal, so everyone around the world can relate to them.

In March 2000, Christina's Miami concert will air on The Disney Channel's 2 Hour Tour, a music documentary series that lets up-and-coming artists perform with established performers like Christina. Christina will also be releasing more singles from her debut album, including the big ballads "I Turn To You" and "So Emotional," accompanied by innovative, exciting videos. She has said she hopes one day to record a duet with her idol, Mariah Carey.

Christina is also doing more writing – she co-wrote "We're A Miracle," which features on the soundtrack to *Pokémon: The First Movie* – and has said that after a busy day she likes to come home, think about the day, and start writing music. She wants to continue to put her stamp on the music business, and has said that the music that is out right now is often focused on the melody or the hook, and not the emotion or real feeling. She has said she especially loves Lauryn Hill because she pours sincere emotion into every note. Christina wants to continue to do the same, and on the evidence of her soaring ballads, she's doing just that.

Christina has said that after a busy day she likes to come home, think about the day, and start writing music.

Christina has also said she'd like to try her hand at producing, and would love to try acting on Broadway, in movies and on television. "I'm very interested in acting, but right now I'm promoting my album and going on tour because that's my first love," she said during a live internet chat. "But I'm very interested in doing some parts that come my way."

When people ask her if the wild world of showbiz has "messed her up" she has responded that she'd be "messed up" if she wasn't following her dreams in music. She has even joked that if she hadn't made it as a singer, she'd like to try working at the window of a drive-thru fast food restaurant. It looks like she chose the right calling with music! Down the line Christina has said she would like to go to college and major in something other than music, like psychology. She also wants to do more work with battered women and children and truly make an impact on the world.

Just like Mariah Carey inspired Christina and others throughout the 1990s, Christina herself is an inspiration for countless girls today. "It's a dream come true. I've wanted this forever – my entire life! So now that it's happening, I'm thrilled," she said during a live internet chat.

Christina Aguilera is changing the face of music and has showed other aspiring singers that you don't need lots of gimmicks and marketing to succeed if you can really sing. She's truly proven that dreams can come true!

Just like Mariah Carey inspired Christina and others throughout the 1990s, Christina herself is an inspiration for countless girls today.

Test Your 'Tina Trivia

How well do you know Christina? Now that you've read all the details about Christina Aguilera, you and a friend can test your Christina IQ with this quiz. Good luck!

1. Christina is learning how to sing in
a. Spanish
b. French
c. Japanese

2. Christina is often compared with
a. Mariah Carey
b. Britney Spears
c. Whitney Houston

3. Christina's drink of choice is
a. Chocolate milk
b. Root beer
c. Orange juice

4. What show did Christina guest star on?
a. *Dawson's Creek*
b. *Beverly Hills 90210*
c. *Ally McBeal*

5. Christina has a crush on
a. Kid Rock
b. Julio Iglesias Jr
c. Enrique Iglesias

6. For what audition did she have to hit the right note, a high E above middle C?
a. *Star Search*
b. *The New Mickey Mouse Club*
c. *Mulan*

7. One of her most treasured childhood gifts was
a. *Barbie kitchen*
b. *Walkman*
c. *Cabbage Patch Kid*

8. What word does Christina use most?
a. Hello
b. Whatever
c. Cute

9. Christina loves wearing clothes by
a. Tommy Hilfiger
b. Dolce & Gabbana
c. BCBG

10. What's Christina's advice for other girls who want to pursue their dream?
a. Find something you're passionate about
b. Work hard and never give up
c. Always follow your heart

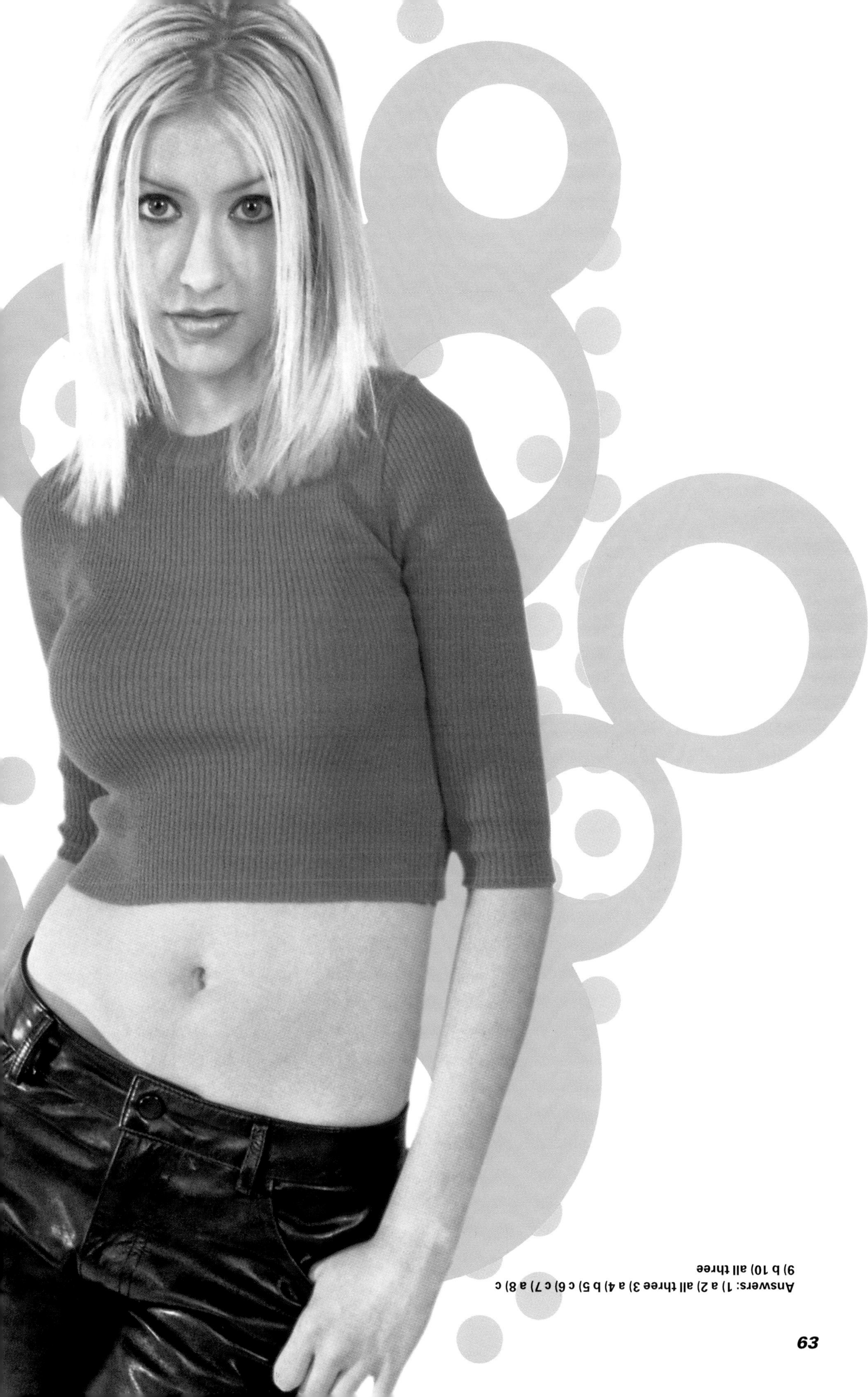

Answers: 1) a 2) all three 3) a 4) b 5) c 6) c 7) a 8) c
9) b 10) all three

Discography

Singles

"Genie In A Bottle"
RCA, Released June 1999
Highest Chart Position: 1

"What A Girl Wants"
RCA, Released December 1999

"The Christmas Song"
RCA, Released December 1999

Albums

Christina Aguilera
RCA, Released August 1999
Highest Chart Position: 1
Genie In A Bottle/What A Girl Wants/I Turn To
You/So Emotional/Come On Over (All I Want Is
You)/Reflection/Love For All
Seasons/Somebody's Somebody/When You Put
Your Hands On Me/Blessed/Love Will Find A
Way/Obvious

Soundtracks

Mulan
Walt Disney Records, Released June 1998
Honor To Us All – Beth Fowler, Marnie Nixon,
Lea Salonga, Chorus/Reflection – Lea Salonga/I'll
Make A Man Out Of You – Donny Osmond,
Chorus/A Girl Worth Fighting For – Harvey
Fierstein, James Hong, Lea Salonga, Jerry
Tondo, Matthew Wilder, Chorus/True To Your
Heart – 98 Degrees, Stevie Wonder/Suite From
"Mulan" – Jerry Goldsmith/Attack At The Wall –
(score) Jerry Goldsmith/Mulan's Decision –
(score) Jerry Goldsmith/Blossoms – (score)
Jerry Goldsmith/The Huns Attack – (score) Jerry
Goldsmith/The Burned-Out Village – (score)
Jerry Goldsmith/Reflection (Pop Version) –
Christina Aguilera

Pokémon: The First Movie
Atlantic, Released November 1999
Pokémon Theme – Billy Crawford/Don't Say You
Love Me – M2M/It Was You – Ashley Ballard
(with So Plush)/We're A Miracle – Christina
Aguilera/Soda Pop – Britney Spears/
Somewhere, Someday – 'N Sync/Get Happy –
B*witched/(Hey You) Free Up Your Mind –
Emma Bunton/Fly With Me – 98
Degrees/Lullaby – Mandah/Vacation – Vitamin
C/Makin' My Way (Any Way That I Can) –
Billie/Catch Me If You Can – Angela Via/Have
Some Fun With The Funk – Aaron Carter/If Only
Tears Could Bring You Back – Midnight
Sons/Brother My Brother – Blessid Union
Of Souls